Ulrike Welsch...

came to America from her native Germany in 1964. The first female staff photographer ever hired by a Boston newspaper, she spent a total of fourteen and a half years working first for the *Boston Herald-Traveler* and later for the *Boston Globe.*

She describes her photography: "I like to make friends with people and photograph life. Sometimes it's a face that speaks to me, sometimes light creating a mood. I seldom know in advance what I will photograph; I always know it when I see it. It will be reachable, a segment out of the everyday scene."

Ulrike Welsch is a frequent contributor to *Time, Life,* and *Yankee* magazines, and her photographs have appeared in such books as *Kids of Colombia, The World I Love To See,* and *A Day in the Life of Australia.* Having taught photojournalism for the past ten years, she currently conducts seminars at Harvard's Center for Lifelong Learning.

Cover photograph:
Jake and Harold Hayward, boiling maple sap
in Chelsea, Vermont.

Cover design:
J Porter

FACES *of* NEW ENGLAND

FACES *of* NEW ENGLAND

Special moments from everyday life.
Photographs & Text by Ulrike Welsch

FROM *YANKEE BOOKS*

A division of Yankee Publishing Incorporated
Dublin, New Hampshire

Acknowledgments

Thank you to everybody who is part of my *Faces of New England.* Thank you also to the participants behind the scenes, the subjects whose photographs were not, in the end, included, but who permitted me to be among them with my camera. And thanks to the friends who helped me with encouragement, ideas, and photo selection throughout the year; to Dr. Jan Fontein of the Boston Museum of Fine Arts; to my editor, Sharon Smith; my designer, J Porter; and the whole Yankee idea.

Thank you, too, to those organizations and individuals whose cooperation led to the photos included here: the Athletic Department of Brown University; Bath Iron Works; the owners and crew of the *Bill of Rights*; Boston's Fish Pier and auctioneers; the Boston Seaman's House; Christians Farm; the Consolidated Cigar Corporation; De Stefano Studio; the First Parish Church of Plymouth; Harvard University; the Hitchcock Chair Factory; Jasper Wyman & Son; Kearsarge Sawmill and Lumber Company; the Kearsarge Theatre; the Marblehead School of Ballet; the Museum of Fine Arts; the Narragansett Indians; Newton Wellesley Hospital; the Penobscot Indians of Old Town, Maine; the Rock of Ages Corporation; Seaview Fillet Company; the Shindiggers; the Skating Club of Boston; and Stinson Canning Company.

Edited by Sharon Smith
Designed by J Porter

Yankee Publishing Incorporated
Dublin, New Hampshire 03444
First Edition

Copyright 1983, Ulrike Welsch

Library of Congress Catalog Card Number: 83-50088
ISBN: 0-89909-015-X (hardcover)
ISBN: 0-89909-017-6 (softcover)

To my subjects and my friends.

Foreword

Those who know the development of the career of Ulrike Welsch may say that she first discovered America and then photography, for if we place the events in her life in their chronological sequence, it would certainly seem to be that way. In the beginning she knew about photography only what any amateur knows. While she obtained some additional skills in what was later to become her trade, this was merely a by-product of her pharmaceutical training in her native Germany. It was only after she came to the New World that she discovered the branch of photography that is known as photojournalism, and it was here in Boston that she began to build a career on the foundations of her one-time hobby.

On the other hand, we could also say that she first discovered photography and then America. For it is obvious to anyone familiar with her work that it was through photography that she began to see America and its people, and that it was photography that provided the impetus for her travels to every corner of New England.

Yet we should not think of Ulrike Welsch as a photographer who sees the world only through the lens or view finder of her camera. Her photographs often have that special effect that only quiet, unobtrusive observation can produce, but never do we feel that element of intrusion that characterizes the photojournalism of the *paparazzi* brand. For even when captured in a moment of spontaneity, the people of New England who appear in this book are always fully aware of her presence. Yet, in spite of this awareness, they are never posed.

I first became aware of Ulrike Welsch's photographs some ten years ago, when they began to appear in the *Boston Globe*. The photographs often related to the specific events that were covered by the newspaper. Yet they always had a character of their own, striking images that revealed a human dimension not contained in the story itself. Sometimes it was as if she had extracted from the situation a whimsical or poetic component, unseen by others but captured by her camera.

As her talent matured and her vision gained in depth she expanded her activities into areas where the daily requirements of photojournalism, which had first stimulated her energy, tend to become constraints. *Faces of New England* is one of the first products of her regained artistic freedom.

Roaming throughout the region she has been fascinated by the people she has seen, the people who display the infinite ethnic and social variety that constitutes the kaleidoscope of New England. Together with her we see them at work and at play, in quiet solitude as well as in places bustling with activity, in moments of intense joy and pride — all of them just being themselves. In short vignettes she tells us where and how she met them, who they are, and what they do.

In her preface she writes how making this book has enriched her life. No wonder that the pleasure with which she worked on this project is contagious and transmitted to us on every page. She may think *Faces of New England* has enriched her life. I think she has enriched ours.

— *Jan Fontein*
Director
Boston Museum of Fine Arts

Preface

The biggest source of enrichment in my life is photojournalism, the career I chose when coming to America from my native Germany.

My newspaper experience in Boston and my travels to South America, Southeast Asia, and Australia have taught me the technique and discipline of my trade, but most of all they have taught me how to move about comfortably with all people. And people are the enrichment.

This last year, after I decided to photograph independently, Yankee Books invited me to gather material about the people of New England. Now I had the opportunity to devote more time to individuals without racing against daily deadlines. Now I could stop and talk, absorb and observe for hours or even days at a time.

A year is a long time, but yet a very short time, to photograph a good selection for a book. For the sake of concentration and of discipline it is better to have a goal and a time limit. Otherwise one never finds an end, never has enough . . . and yes, New Englanders are such a varied breed.

I threw myself into many different situations, sometimes carefully planning the days, other times photographing everyday scenes at random. Each day was a search for the ultimate. I found fulfillment, and I found frustrating disappointment. For in photojournalism nothing is certain; it may be the people, the light, even me. There is constant change.

I enjoyed photographing alone, roaming New England with my dog and my VW "bug." Along the 20,000 miles of this past year's travels, I constantly searched for pictures of everyday life: joy, sadness, work, play. I chose the people who appealed to me most — those I could talk to, those who let me come in, who let me be a photographing "mouse" among them. If I was not wanted, I did not want. I tried to reason and persuade for a little while, but never to press. My time is precious, and so very precious when people are themselves, "do their thing," react, interact, and forget about me. I would click away, stepping around them discreetly, imagining that if I stepped more slowly they would not see or feel me. They always knew my presence, though. Or almost always — there were only a few like Madas, who didn't see me until after I had clicked fifteen times while she said her morning prayers.

Looking back now, after 329 rolls of New England, I have seen and learned much anew. I have seen a bill being figured the old-fashioned way on a woman's hand, I've joined the camaraderie backstage at a country theatre, I've seen a granite quarry in full swing. I've visited the bone chamber of a private museum, gained insight into life on an Indian reservation, followed the earthy routine of a country vet, learned all about tobacco growing, and met many whose work and life is the sea.

I have learned much during this year's wanderings, but of course no book about New England could be large enough to show everything. The photographs selected here are impressions from a time of searching — only my favorite faces and experiences remain.

— *Ulrike Welsch*

**FANEUIL HALL,
BOSTON,
MASSACHUSETTS**

Once or twice a month,
about 350 natives of foreign
lands stand in Boston's Faneuil Hall. Each raises his
right hand, gives up his old
citizenship, and takes the
oath to become a United
States citizen. Some are
older, some are young; some
have waited for the mini-
mum five years after coming
here and some eighteen.
Each holds a little American
flag in his hand or wears it
pinned to his collar. At the
end of this simple ceremony,
they all pledge allegiance to
the flag. It is an impressive
moment. It gave me goose
pimples.

12

**OAK BLUFFS,
MARTHA'S VINEYARD, MASSACHUSETTS**
Every summer Winfield S. Smith, now in his late
nineties, hangs his flag out in front of his house. The
house is part of the Martha's Vineyard Camp Meeting
Association and, like the other houses in the association, it is just covered with "gingerbread." The
neighborhood has its own church, its own tabernacle
for chorus and concert performances, and its own
rules: most roads within the association are off limits
to cars and bicycles. The older folks here like the
quiet life and enjoy watching the neighborhood from
their porch rocking chairs.

CORNISH, NEW HAMPSHIRE
He sells popcorn at the Cornish Fair—
and likes to eat it, too!

WOONSOCKET, RHODE ISLAND

BOSTON,
MASSACHUSETTS

"My daddy makes music. He is King Wellington. He plays Calypso, he makes whole songs, and then he sings and swings. When I am with my daddy, I want to dance all the time. He makes my toes tickle—my whole body wants to wiggle."

—*Kahille Quashie*

BOSTON, MASSACHUSETTS
"Don't laugh. I lost my baby teeth."

MARBLEHEAD, MASSACHUSETTS
Best friends.

WARNER, NEW HAMPSHIRE
Justin and Nathan.

CHELSEA, VERMONT
Mary Ellen.

CAMBRIDGE, MASSACHUSETTS
Harvard commencement.

CAMBRIDGE, MASSACHUSETTS
Harvard commencement.

CAMBRIDGE, MASSACHUSETTS
A little music from the underclassmen.

**CAMBRIDGE,
MASSACHUSETTS**
No shade in Harvard Yard.

CLASS DAY PRO
JUNE 9, 1982, 2:00 P.M.

**BOSTON,
MASSACHUSETTS**

The light was dim at the John Collins Warren Anatomical Museum, but my eyes traveled and discovered much around David Gunner. There was lots to see — more than the books this man was immersed in. I saw models of organs, instruments, an arm bone, a set of teeth and, yes, skulls of many shapes and sizes.

Mr. Gunner, director of this private professional anatomical museum at Harvard Medical School, gave me a gracious and informative tour of his department. The museum has an immense collection of specimens, artifacts, and memorabilia of physicians and surgeons from the eighteenth, nineteenth, and twentieth centuries. We went to the bone chamber, then to rooms full of cases and drawers containing specimens all labeled and catalogued.

David Gunner does research, documentation, and restoration, as well as preparing exhibits and sometimes participating in group lectures. I was happy he found time for me, even letting me use his tripod to steady my camera in the minimal light. This man radiates so much knowledge, but he never let me feel inadequate.

30

MARBLEHEAD, MASSACHUSETTS

If you are looking for a good beard, Floyd Soule is the man to seek. He even gives you a choice of how *much* beard. When we first got acquainted, Floyd's beard was moderately short. "There is more to it, you know. Want me to get all of it out?" Not knowing what he meant, I left it at that until we really got down to photographing. Again he offered more beard. This time I dared. And here, tucked away beneath Floyd's T-shirt, was all the rest, which he had not cut in five years. The beard is multicolored — though once, in Japan, a barber dyed it solid purple by mistake.

Floyd Soule is a busy man. He has his friends, a few chickens, his books, and Mrs. Soule. She just came home. In goes the beard . . . .

MUSEUM OF FINE ARTS, BOSTON, MASSACHUSETTS
True art is holding six brushes in one hand.

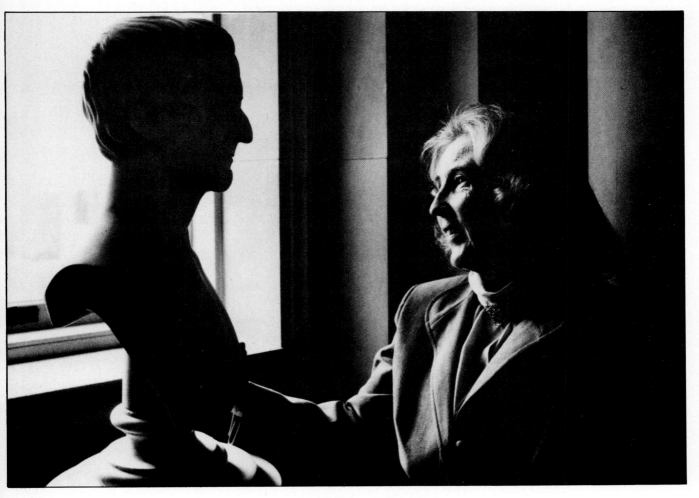

NEWPORT, RHODE ISLAND

There were statues everywhere, including one of Nicolas Brown, Mrs. Eileen G. Slocum's great grandfather. There was an outstanding female bust near the door, so perfect that I couldn't resist blowing at the marble veil to see if it would move. The Slocums have lived here since 1953, and treasures have accumulated. It's not a simple home, but it's very livable, with geraniums over the washing machine and a rack holding the delights of a very hat-loving family.

WOBURN, MASSACHUSETTS
Fiber glass Christmas decorations for Bloomingdale's, coming out of the sand-blasting chamber.

34

SALEM, MASSACHUSETTS
A witches' séance.

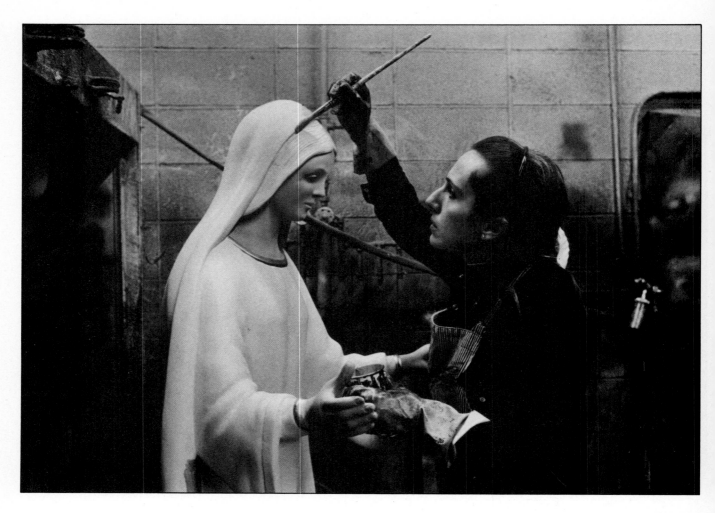

WOBURN, MASSACHUSETTS
At the mannequin factory.

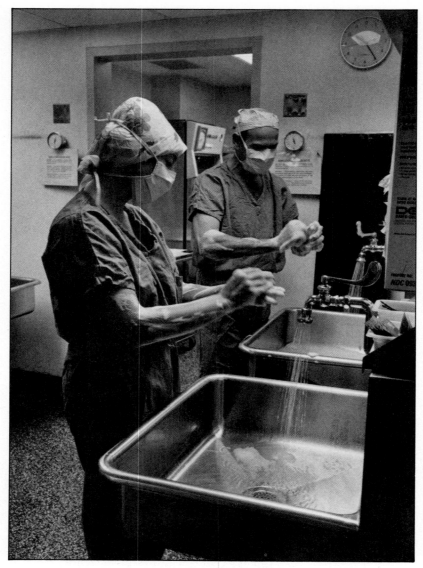

NEWTON LOWER FALLS, MASSACHUSETTS

It was my night to watch the babies arrive at Newton Wellesley Hospital. Three women in early labor walked the hall of the maternity ward, pacing heavily and slowly. Suddenly, without much warning, everything started to happen at once. Nurses and doctors—prepared, of course—were rushing about; they wheeled in a Russian lady, and within what seemed minutes the couple had their first child born on American soil. I remember the beautiful hands the woman had, the beautiful rings she wore—and the wonderfully expressive baby she bore.

I had to hurry to catch all the arrivals. Each time it was an amazing moment when a whole little person appeared, with tiny eyes that looked around and an amazingly big voice that gave that first yell.

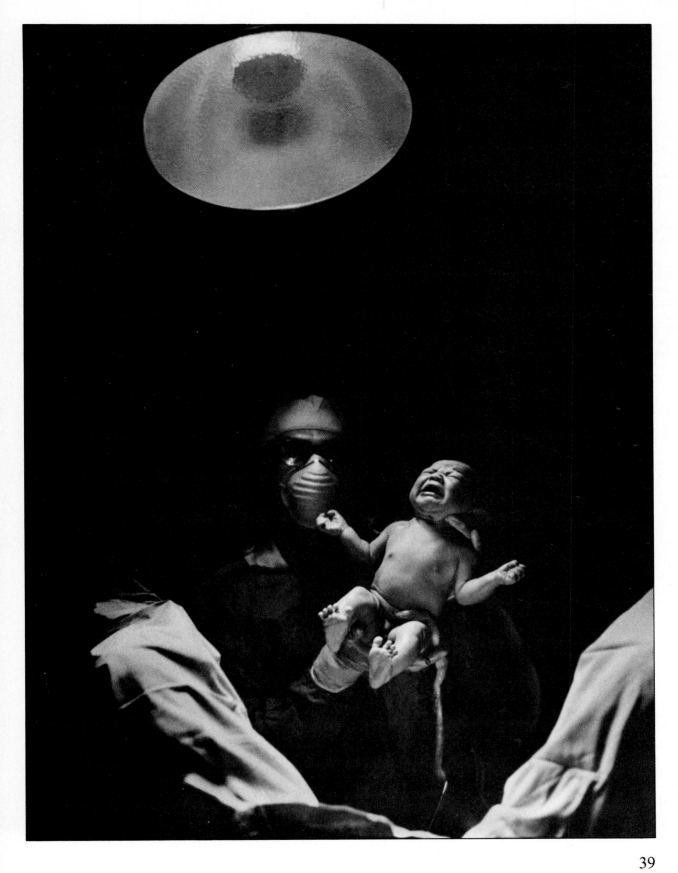

EASTERN POINT LIGHT, GLOUCESTER, MASSACHUSETTS

"Clear 10 miles, west 10 knots, seas 01-02, 18, 30.34 pressure, wind chill -9." That was one of the eight reports a day that lighthouse keeper Michael Mone called in to the weather station. Except for one other nearby lighthouse family, Michael Mone, Sheila, Timmy, and Maura are virtually alone. The two households share shopping trips and, sometimes, much more — together they have weathered storms with winds from the northeast gusting up to seventy knots, and normally ten-foot tides rising to fifteen feet high.

NEW LONDON, CONNECTICUT

Mack Lucas is the elevator operator at the Mercer
Building, where lots of clients and employees go in and
out all day. "Here comes Miss Hollywood. Welcome to
this elevator!" And up they go. On his lunch hour,
Mack paints scenes from magazines and postcards onto
wood, cardboard, paper scraps, the old propeller at the
railroad station — whatever he has. Once an architect
who works in the building rescued and framed a fishing
scene that Mack had tossed into the wastebasket.

ABBOT HALL,
MARBLEHEAD, MASSACHUSETTS

ABBOT HALL,
MARBLEHEAD, MASSACHUSETTS
Admiring *The Spirit of '76.*

43

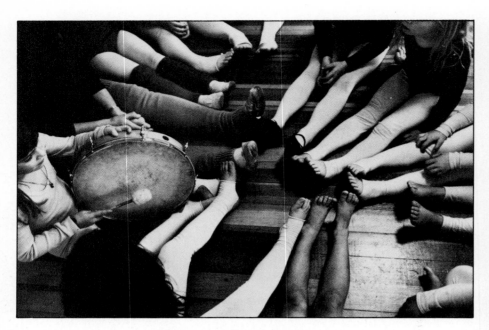

**MARBLEHEAD SCHOOL OF BALLET,
MARBLEHEAD, MASSACHUSETTS**
A class for creative movement.

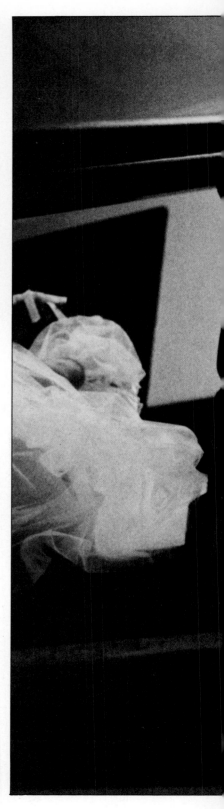

MARBLEHEAD, MASSACHUSETTS
Tanya.

45

WARNER, NEW HAMPSHIRE

It was the last play of the season at the Kearsarge Theatre (known in its other life as the Warner Town Hall).
Margery, the lead, had brought a gift for everyone in
the women's locker room. They knew each other well
now; camaraderie had knit them together. In the mirror I saw someone stripping—nothing mattered now
except speed. "Does anyone have an extra pair of nylons? I ripped mine." "I'll curl your hair, you do your
eyes." "Debby, can I have your mascara for a minute?"

WARNER, NEW HAMPSHIRE
Warming up, they were nearly ready to become *Guys and Dolls.*

BRIGHTON, MASSACHUSETTS
The skating club's seventieth birthday began with a
Dutch waltz.

DANVERS, MASSACHUSETTS
The caller gave the directions: do-si-do, square
through, load the boat, teacup chain, chase right.
All the Shindiggers knew their commands; they turned
and chased, laughed and swung. Petticoats rustled,
and once in a while a kiss was exchanged in a turn.

NORTH END,
BOSTON, MASSACHUSETTS
The Feast of Saint Anthony.

NORTH END, BOSTON, MASSACHUSETTS
At the corner of Salem Street.

STARK, NEW HAMPSHIRE
At the fiddlers' contest.

CRAFTSBURY, VERMONT
Getting in tune for the
banjo contest.

54

STARK, NEW HAMPSHIRE

**STERLING,
MASSACHUSETTS**
Queen Anne's lace.

56

STARK, NEW HAMPSHIRE
Even my camera was dancing—
but always clicking.

CRAFTSBURY, VERMONT

EXETER, NEW HAMPSHIRE

WARNER, NEW HAMPSHIRE

PROVIDENCE, RHODE ISLAND
Brown's Homecoming game. Dartmouth won.

REVERE, MASSACHUSETTS
Partybound on Halloween.

NEWPORT, RHODE ISLAND
While the *Valdez* was in port, many sailors were on
leave. At the No Name the pool was good, and on
Wednesday from 8 to 10 the beer was free.

MACHIAS, MAINE
The letter is written to Santa—little Laura Crockett,
barely able to write, wants a motorcycle!

MACHIAS, MAINE
Laura.

PROSPECT HARBOR, MAINE
George Lowell used to go out to sea. Now he lets the young do the work, but he still gets together with them outside the sardine factory. There he catches up on all the news and invites good friends to help celebrate his fiftieth wedding anniversary at the community house.

WARNER, NEW HAMPSHIRE
George Dame has a shingle splitting business. Helen
Smith cooks and takes care of him—and of Brownie.
Their small, shingled house is all secured for winter
and quite warm inside because of Helen's cooking.

WASHINGTON, MAINE
Now that the beans have been snapped. . . .

70

LENOX, MASSACHUSETTS
Supper at Tanglewood.

BOSTON CITY HALL,
BOSTON, MASSACHUSETTS

Following her husband, who had found work here,
Caretha Brown came to Boston from Georgia about
twenty years ago. She bore seventeen children (twelve
are living) and has more than twenty-five grandchildren and two great grandchildren. Her children say
she is the mother of the city of Boston.

Twice a week Mother Brown, as she is affectionately
called, tends the main gallery at City Hall as a volunteer. She loves to dress up and loves to sing in the
choir at New Hope Baptist Church on Tremont Street.
And she loves to philosophize. "It all will come as the
good Lord wants it. We ought to understand one another," she says. She doesn't worry about anything.

EAST RANDOLPH, VERMONT
The years have gone by, and the heifers have all been sold now.

73

**PROVIDENCE,
RHODE ISLAND**
Even the barber needs a
shave sometimes.

BOSTON, MASSACHUSETTS
At the Boston Seaman's House.

MARBLEHEAD, MASSACHUSETTS

Before Lincoln Hawkes was born in 1923, his father used to sit by the fireplace reading his two older boys stories about Abraham Lincoln. The family was hoping for a baby girl and planning to call her Sally. But the baby's due date was February 12, so with all that reading in mind, Linc's father decided that if the baby were a boy, they could call him Lincoln. "I fooled the old man twice," Linc says today. He wasn't the expected girl, and he was born on Valentine's Day instead of Lincoln's Birthday—but they called him Lincoln anyway.

SAINT JOHNSBURY, VERMONT

Washday for Ralph Bridges—his wife was ill.

WARNER, NEW HAMPSHIRE
Ready to leap off the Joppa Bridge.

MYSTIC, CONNECTICUT

STARK, NEW HAMPSHIRE
South Pond.

CHERRYFIELD, MAINE

For most of the year Rosi Francis, a native American, lives on a reservation in Big Cove, New Brunswick, with little opportunity to earn money for clothes and better food. But during blueberry harvest time, she, her son, and much of her family lived out of a large blue truck at the edge of Strawberry Patch, the campground for migrant workers. They washed, cooked, ate, and played chess beneath the open skies. And from six or seven in the morning until the sun was too high and hot, they stood with their backs bent, raking the "blue gold."

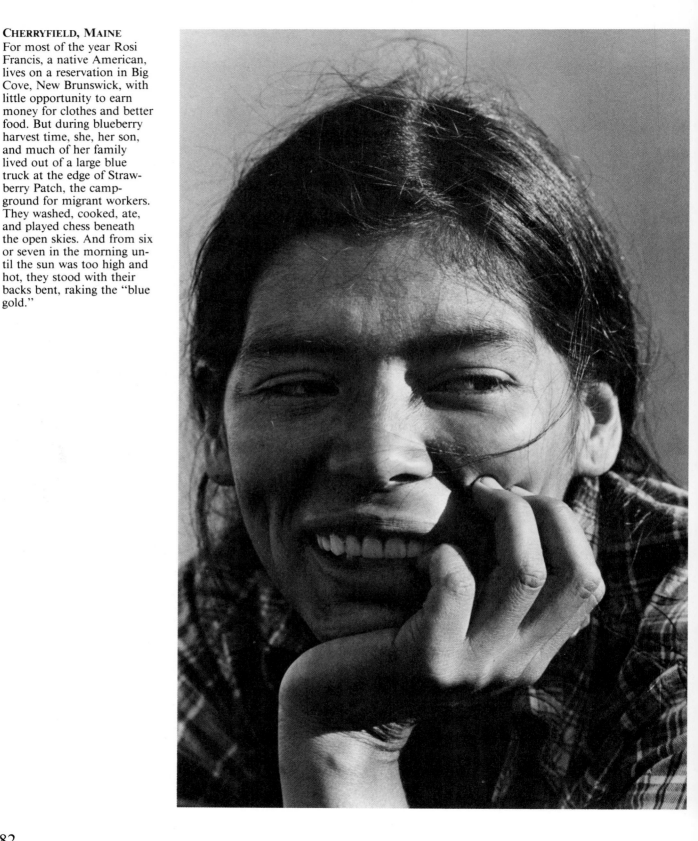

CHARLESTOWN, RHODE ISLAND
Princess Moon Glove.

OLD TOWN, MAINE

In 1904 her parents named her Madas, meaning "last baby." Later, when she was at Wounded Knee in 1972, she called herself a revolutionary. Out west she is known as "The Prayer Lady." And back home on Indian Island, the doctor said she will be the healthiest woman on the reservation if she watches her sugar and gets her weight down.

I met Madas at 4:30 AM, during her morning prayers, and again at 11 PM, when she had just refused a dinner of baked beans and hot dogs. In between, whether she was shopping with her son Bobcat, going to church with her friends, or attending the council meeting in the main house, she radiated wisdom and a broadmindedness that went beyond Old Town, where the Penobscots settled before the white man came.

CHARLESTOWN, RHODE ISLAND
Lloyd Wilcox, from Putnam, Connecticut, dressed in his medicine man garb to lead the ceremonies during the annual Thanksgiving celebration. He consulted with others—mostly direct descendants of the Narragansett tribe—in namegiving, then danced and shared both peace pipe and food.

MEDWAY, MASSACHUSETTS

SALISBURY, NEW HAMPSHIRE

It was in December that Laura shoed April. Laura Hamilton, the most petite blacksmith in the Concord area, has a way with horses. If April was nervous, because she was a young horse, Laura knew how to soothe her.

Laura, who has been on her own for six years now, is known to a wide community of horse owners. Her little red van with the anvil in the rear, her mild voice, and her tender touch with horses are welcome everywhere—even with the men.

CORNISH, NEW HAMPSHIRE

CORNISH, NEW HAMPSHIRE
At the Cornish Fair.

NEAR EXETER, NEW HAMPSHIRE

It was rounds day with veterinarian Bob Marsten, and he had an early call to check a cow with mastitis in East Kingston. Fourteen gallons of water were put down her throat with the help of a tube, a hose, and lots of hands. When they were finished everybody just walked away, leaving the cow in the hay. Their caring didn't show.

Later we picked up a ewe and took it with us in the van to Dr. Marsten's veterinary clinic in Amesbury, Massachusetts. The ewe was pregnant, and it had a tumor growing inward beneath its shoulder. But Number 8017 was a happy and curious ewe, looking at the sights during the ride and even in the operating room till the sedative injection took effect. The tumor had penetrated deeply, but the operation went well and the ewe was quickly stitched up.

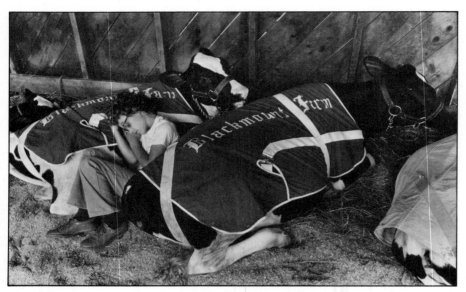

CORNISH, NEW HAMPSHIRE
Catnap for Samantha.

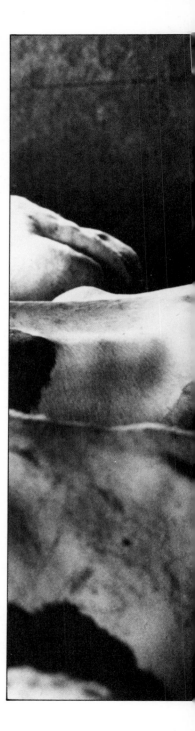

MERRIMAC, MASSACHUSETTS
Bruce Kaiser has been a herdsman for more than
twenty years on the Cobblers Brook Farm. The cows
have become his life—and his friends.

**CONTOOCOOK,
NEW HAMPSHIRE**

When I first went to meet
Robert Mock, I really had to
holler into the woods—I
didn't want a tree to come
down on me! He was busy
with his chainsaw and his
logs and wasn't watching for
the "billy goat," as he called
me later when he saw me
climbing on the rough and
snowy terrain.

Robert Mock amazed me. He sawed, bent, threw the
logs, hitched up his oxen, and commanded them. He
told me that he had been a champion arm wrestler
until two years ago—and that he had once "wheelbar-
rowed" a Volkswagen and its driver to a garage single-
handedly. Today he cuts and loads on his truck a cord
and a half of wood a day. His youngest boys, ages nine
and eleven, already manage their own oxen during
school vacations. They have learned from their father
to guide the three-and-a-half-ton giants with just a tap
of the whip, just a click of the tongue.

CHELSEA, VERMONT
Harold Hayward has boiled maple sap for half a century, his son Jake ever since he was big enough to help. They farm, too, but in March and early April their main interest is sugaring. All morning it rained, and Jake couldn't go into the woods to collect the sap. So the men fired and boiled and tested the syrup inside the sugar house until condensation made it rain there, too.

GRANVILLE, MASSACHUSETTS
Ralph Hiers is the grandson of the founder of the Noble and Cooley Toy and Drum Factory and has worked there since 1926. But in 1976 he built his own Mill in the Meadow and now, since he is officially retired from the factory, he seems to get busier all the time. The mill — even the working water wheel — is entirely his own design, and he's very proud of it.

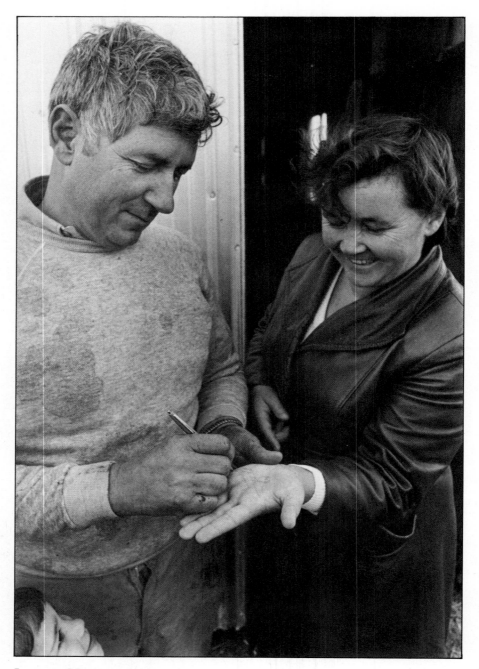

IPSWICH, MASSACHUSETTS
Mario Marini grows cabbage and potatoes, and in the
fall he presses cider; I found him sorting apples as
they tumbled toward the press. Later the Olesches,
from Dorchester, came by as they have for many
years because they like Mario, his potatoes, and his
cabbage. And they like the way he writes his bills, the
old-fashioned way, on Antonina Olesch's hand.

SHEFFIELD, VERMONT
A Sunday ride with Toto.

NEW HARBOR, MAINE
The scarecrow, he told me,
was his friend.

BRADFORD, NEW HAMPSHIRE

107

BARRE, VERMONT
Coffee break.

WARNER, NEW HAMPSHIRE
A log scaler.

SUFFIELD, CONNECTICUT

At Christian Farms I found about 150 young people, aged fourteen to eighteen, helping to harvest the tobacco crop at the end of their summer vacations. Some of the boys rushed about beneath the tents, peering with trained eyes, placing just the ripe leaves in the baskets. Others, collecting the baskets, took them by tractor to the barn, where the girls threaded the leaves, and other helpers and the owners stowed them far aloft.

Tobacco leaves, especially the shade-grown kind, must be treated carefully; one leaf of "shade" wraps up to eight cigars, and unbroken leaves bring the most money. Everybody knows the rules, so not much gets lost — and I heard lots of teasing and laughter.

112

HAZARDVILLE, CONNECTICUT

"¿Habla Español?" Si, I could, and I climbed onto the truck. Most of those who gather broadleaf tobacco in the fields of Consolidated Cigars are Spanish-speaking. And most, like Felix Santiago, who tacked the cut tobacco plants up to dry, live in Springfield, Massachusetts.

CHERRYFIELD, MAINE
Winnowing the blueberries.

CHERRYFIELD, MAINE
Sorting frozen blueberries.

PINKHAM NOTCH, NEW HAMPSHIRE
William.

PINKHAM NOTCH, NEW HAMPSHIRE

PINKHAM NOTCH, NEW HAMPSHIRE
Tuckerman Ravine

MANCHESTER-BY-THE-SEA, MASSACHUSETTS

EDGARTOWN,
MARTHA'S VINEYARD, MASSACHUSETTS
Hitch a ride — meet a stranger.

SALEM, MASSACHUSETTS
During the week, Bernie van Knowe is a plumbing
contractor, but on weekends he loves to scuba dive. At
forty feet he digs for quahogs; at sixty and seventy feet
he harpoons flounder and looks for lobsters. Over the
years he has found treasures small and large: bottles in
all shapes, beautifully decorated with coral growth,
and a seven-foot-tall anchor, dating from approxi-
mately 1700, which now decorates his hallway.

CHAPPAQUIDDICK,
MARTHA'S VINEYARD, MASSACHUSETTS

WOODS HOLE, MASSACHUSETTS
Ever since her girlhood in South Carolina, she's
been fishing.

Overleaf:
ROCKPORT, MASSACHUSETTS

PROVINCETOWN, MASSACHUSETTS
Christine.

129

FALMOUTH, MASSACHUSETTS

BOOTHBAY HARBOR, MAINE
Watching the windjammer parade.

OFF BLOCK ISLAND, RHODE ISLAND
Vacation on the *Bill of Rights.*

BOOTHBAY HARBOR, MAINE
Tabor Boy.

FRIENDSHIP, MAINE

A thirty-two-foot wooden sloop was being built in the
boatyard of Winfield Lash, one of the most camera
shy but also most hospitable men I've ever met. I
watched as his brother, Harold, and ship's carpenter,
Joel, prepared the planks to be bent and fitted, then
followed Winfield Lash on a tour of his shed filled
with old ships' engines and a workroom holding the
blueprints of all the boats he has built and is now
planning. Among those future plans is an eighty-foot
wooden sailboat with a small motor, to be used for
fishing. Before he can build a boat that big, he'll have
to extend his loft so the new boat, like all his others,
can slip right into the bay.

BATH, MAINE

WALDOBORO, MAINE

When her children were young, Sheila Fowler moved
to Maine so they could grow up away from the city.
She opened Sheila's Shanty next door to her home
and started shucking clams for restaurants and for special orders. Today her daughter-in-law Kathleen works
with her. During the day all kinds of people stop by
— friends, clammers, the kids. Chatting with them,
shucking clams, and serving on the local volunteer
ambulance team keep her busy, and Sheila is pleased
that the clam shanty and the ambulance team have
given her a strong link to the community.

NEW BEDFORD, MASSACHUSETTS
Coffee break at the fillet factory.

PROSPECT HARBOR, MAINE
Sardine canners snip up to twenty-five cases (each containing one hundred cans) of sardines a day. Their hands work quickly with small, sharp scissors — that's why their fingers are taped.

BOSTON, MASSACHUSETTS
At a fish auction.

MARBLEHEAD, MASSACHUSETTS
After the rain.

SOUTH BRISTOL, MAINE

Brown net studded with corks flowed all around "Biscuit" when we met at the town pier on Rutherford Island, and his two-day-old beard sparkled with silver. I wanted to photograph Harold McFarland, so I told him, outright, that I liked his looks. He said, "You aren't too bad either!" (Well, it was summertime.)

Biscuit sat in the middle of the netting, pulled out a beer, had a sip, and talked. And we did get along. Telling one tale after another, he explained that his nickname had been given to him when he was a child in honor of his favorite food. Before I left, Biscuit signed my model release, using my back as a table. But then in big letters he wrote "Biscuit" on my skin, for me to keep as a souvenir.

I couldn't wash for days!

143